Modern Mersey Shipping

by

Ian Collard

The **Balmoral** (BHS, 43,537gt/88) was built by Jos L Meyer, Papenburg, Germany. She is owned by Fred Olsen Cruise Lines Limited. She was built as **Crown Odyssey** for the Royal Cruise Line, which was acquired by Klosters in 1990, and taken over by the Norwegian Cruise Line in 1996 when she was renamed **Norwegian Crown**. She was transferred to the Orient Line in 2000 as **Crown Odyssey**, but was returned to the Norwegian Cruise Line in 2003 and became **Norwegian Crown** again. In 2007 she was purchased by Fred Olsen and sent to Blohm & Voss at Hamburg where a new 30 metre section was fitted prior to her entering service for the company. We see the **Balmoral** berthed at the Pier Head in Liverpool.

INTRODUCTION

In recent years, the port of Liverpool has experienced a renaissance both in cargo operations and also in the number of passengers using the new Cruise Facility at the Pier Head. The port now handles over 30 million tonnes of cargo every year, serving over 100 destinations around the world. In October 2012 it was awarded Port Authority of the year in the Containerisation International Awards. The capacity at the Royal Seaforth container terminal was expanded in 2012 with the addition of an extra 5,000 ground slots. The steel terminal at Gladstone Dock received a £3 million upgrade.

The new Liverpool Cruise Facility was opened at the Pier Head in 2008 when it attracted 13 calls from cruise liners visiting ports in the Irish Sea. Such vessels offering cruises from the port sailed from Langton Dock within the dock system. Following a campaign, permission was granted to allow voyages to start from the Pier Head Terminal in 2013 when it was agreed to repay the large public subsidy provided for the new terminal. There will be 52 calls at the terminal in 2014.

Work on a new £350 million deepwater container terminal commenced in 2013. It will enable vessels capable of carrying 13,500 TEUs to berth on the Mersey. Currently the port handles container ships with a capacity of 3,000 TEUs. It is claimed that it will transform global supply routes into and out of the UK. The development will create 5,000 jobs and will bring the world's largest container ships to the Mersey. It will be called Liverpool 2 and is due to open in 2015.

Coastal services across the Irish Sea are provided by Stena Line, P&O and Seatruck, all using modern roll-on/roll-off ferries. Stena Line provides car, freight and passenger services using **Stena Lagan** and **Stena Mersey** which have been completely refurbished for the route between Birkenhead and Belfast. Seatruck offers a passenger, car, freight and passenger service with a fleet of modern purpose-built vessels which are the youngest on the Irish Sea. P&O uses a fleet of three vessels sailing to Dublin from its berth in Gladstone Dock. There is also the well-known and popular service to Douglas, Isle of Man, using the fast craft **Manannan** in summer and **Ben-my-chree** in winter.

Although the classic cargo liners have long disappeared from the river and there have been massive changes to the infrastructure within the docks, there is no doubt that the Mersey continues to provide a huge amount of maritime interest. This book aims to reflect the wide variety of vessels that have been seen on the river over the last decade, a variety that has been increased by the search for oil and gas in the Irish Sea and the more recent development of wind farms.

For the information of readers not familiar with it, the information in brackets after the name of the vessel is an abbreviated form of the flag followed by the gross tonnage and then the year of build. I wish to thank Gil Mayes for checking early drafts of the book and the Amadeus Press for their fine work in bringing this book to a successful conclusion.

Ian Collard   Wirral   September 2013

Published by Bernard McCall, 400 Nore Road, Portishead, Bristol, BS20 8EZ, England. Website: www.coastalshipping.co.uk
Telephone/fax: 01275 846178   E-mail: bernard@coastalshipping.co.uk   All distribution enquiries should be addressed to the publisher.

Printed by Amadeus Press, Ezra House, West 26 Business Park, Cleckheaton, West Yorkshire, BD19 4TQ, England. Website: www.amadeuspress.co.uk
Telephone: 01274 863210   Fax: 01274 863211   E-mail: info@amadeuspress.co.uk

ISBN: 978-1-902953-60-1

Front cover: The **Aida Aura** (42289/03) was built at the Aker yard in Wismar, Germany. She is owned by Aida Cruises, Germany. In September 1999 P&O and Seatours formed Aida Cruises to provide a service to the German cruise market. The original vessel, **Aida**, was later joined by two new sisterships which were registered in London. Following the merger of P&O Princess and the Carnival Corporation, the vessels were placed under the control and management of Costa Cruises and the ships were registered in Genoa. **Aida Aura** is accompanied by the **Royal Daffodil** which we see again on page 8.

Back cover: The **Queen Elizabeth** (BMU, 90901gt/10) was built by Fincantieri at Monfalcone, Italy. She is owned by the Cunard Line. **Queen Elizabeth** is a modified Vista class vessel and entered service on 11 October 2010, after being named by Her Majesty The Queen, at Southampton on the previous day. She sailed on her maiden voyage to Vigo, Lisbon, Cadiz, Gran Canaria, Tenerife, La Palma and Madeira. **Queen Elizabeth** is seen here at the Liverpool Cruise Terminal on 8 September 2011 on her maiden Round Britain cruise.

The **Queen Victoria** (BMU, 90049gt/07) was built by Fincantieri at Monfalcone, Italy. She is owned by the Cunard Line. The cruise ship **Arcadia** was originally ordered as **Queen Victoria**, but was delivered as the P&O vessel. The Cunarder's keel was laid at Monfalcone in May 2006, and she was floated out of the dock the following January. She was named by Her Royal Highness The Duchess of Cornwall on 10 December 2007 at Southampton. There is accommodation for 1,990 passengers and 981 crew and she incorporates the Queens Room, Grills, The Royal Spa, Royal Court Theatre and a fitness and treatment room. She berthed at the Liverpool Cruise Facility for the first time on 26 July 2010.

The **Queen Mary 2** (BMU, 148528gt/03) was built at Ateliers et Chantiers de l'Atlantique, St Nazaire, France. **Queen Mary 2** is the flagship of the Cunard Line and here we see her swinging in the river off Seacombe in 2011. She incorporates 14 decks, large public areas, a planetarium, the Royal Court Theatre, Queens Room, library and several recreational areas. She is five times longer than Cunard's first ship, the **Britannia**, 113 feet longer than the original **Queen Mary** and has accommodation for 2,620 passengers and 1,253 crew.

The **Azamara Journey** (MLT, 30277gt/02) was built by Ateliers et Chantiers de l'Atlantique, St Nazaire, France. She was built as **R Six** for Renaissance Cruises which collapsed in 2001 when she was subsequently laid up at Gibraltar with the other seven units of the fleet. She was chartered by Pullmantur Cruises for the 2003-4 seasons and given the name **Blue Star**. She was eventually purchased by them in 2005, becoming **Blue Dream**. Following operation in Brazil she returned to Europe when Pullmantur was purchased by Royal Caribbean in 2006, and it was intended to move her to the Celebrity Expeditions Line with the name **Celebrity Journey**. However, it was decided to place her with Azamara Cruises in the USA as **Azamara Journey**. She pulls away from the Cruise Terminal at Liverpool Pier Head on 22 August 2010.

The **Ocean Countess** (PRT, 17593gt/76) was built by Burmeister & Wain, Copenhagen. She is owned by Majestic International Cruises Inc., Mediterranean Classic Cruises, Greece. She was built for the Cunard Line as **Cunard Countess** and became **Awani Dream 2** in 1996, **Olympic Countess** in 1998, **Olympia Countess** in 2002, **Ocean Countess** in 2004, **Lili Marleen** in 2005, and **Ocean Countess** again in 2006, **Ruby** in 2007 and **Ocean Countess** from 2007. She was designed and built for Cunard's Caribbean cruising programme and was christened at San Juan in August 1976, by Janet Armstrong, wife of Neil Armstrong, the first man to walk on the moon. In 1982, following the conclusion of the Falklands conflict, she was chartered by the Ministry of Defence and carried troops between Ascension Island and Port Stanley. Following an extensive refit in Malta she returned to Caribbean cruising in 1983. She left Cunard ownership in 1996 and has had several owners since, cruising from various ports in Asia and the Mediterranean. In 2012 she was operating cruises from various UK ports on charter to Cruise & Maritime Voyages. These were operated by Discovery in 2013. We see her leaving the River Mersey on a cruise to the Mediterranean.

The World (BHS, 43188gt/02) was built at Bruce's Shipyard, Landskrona. She is owned by Residen Sea Ltd, Norway. We see her berthed at the Liverpool Cruise Facility on 18 August 2010. Her hull was built at Bruce's Shipyard and was then towed to the Fosen Yard at Rissa, in Norway where the vessel was completed. She is the first luxury apartment ship where apartments are sold, with some available for rent. *The World* incorporates 106 two and three bedroom apartments, 19 one and two bedroom studio apartments and 40 studios. The owners of the apartments live on board while the ship sails around the world staying at ports for a couple of days. There is an elected board of residents who advise the company on itinerary and the operation and management of the shop, boutique, gym, tennis court, running track, restaurants, theatre and library.

The *Saga Pearl II* (18627/81) was built at Howaldtswerke-Deutsche Werft, Hamburg, Germany. She was laid down as *Hammonia* for the Hadag Cruise Line and delivered as *Astor*. The South African Marine Corporation acquired her in 1984 to be employed on a Cape Town to Southampton service and planned to use her for cruising when not required on the liner service. However, she was sold to VEB Deutfracht Seereederei of East Germany the following year, replacing *Volkerfreundschaft* and was renamed *Arkona*. She was renamed *Astoria* in 2002 on a ten-year charter, and was purchased by Club Cruise in 2007, but it was anticipated that she would be sold to the Saga Group. However, the sale was cancelled when it was discovered that she had problems with her machinery. Club Cruise was soon placed into administration and *Astoria* was under arrest at Barcelona. The ship was purchased by Saga at an auction at Gibraltar and was sent to Swansea for a £20 million overhaul, emerging as *Saga Pearl II* in 2010. We see her at the Liverpool Cruise Terminal. In 2012 she was renamed *Quest for Adventure*.

Owned by Princess Cruise Lines Ltd, the **Crown Princess** (BMU, 113651gt/06) was built in two sections. The aft section was constructed at the Fincantieri yard in Monfalcone while the forward section came from the Sestri yard in Genoa. She departed from New York on her maiden voyage on 14 June 2006. Just over a month later, on 18 July, a mistake by one of her officers caused a severe list which resulted in almost 300 passengers and crew being injured. The company's website says she can accommodate 3080 passengers although registers note a capacity of 3782. She has a crew of 1185. **Crown Princess** offers 7, 10 and 20-day voyages from Fort Lauderdale and Galveston, and southern, western and eastern Caribbean cruises in the winter. She also offered cruises to the Mediterranean, Scandinavia, northern Europe and around the British Isles in the summer. **Crown Princess** swings in the River Mersey off the Pier Head.

The **Black Watch** (28613gt/72), seen at the Liverpool Cruise Terminal was built at the Wärtsilä shipyard in Helsinki. She was originally built as **Royal Viking Star** for the Royal Viking Line, which was a joint project between an American businessman and three Norwegian shipping companies, including Kloster Cruises, the owner of Norwegian Cruise Line. Three ships offered luxury worldwide cruises and **Royal Viking Star** was followed by **Royal Viking Sky** and **Royal Viking Sea** in 1973. She was lengthened by 27.77 metres at Bremerhaven in 1981, increasing her passenger capacity to 829, and the line was acquired by Kloster Cruises three years later. **Royal Viking Star** was transferred to the Norwegian Cruise Line in 1991, becoming **Westward** and was employed cruising from New York to Bermuda and the Caribbean. In 1994 she became **Star Odyssey** operating in the Mediterranean for the Royal Cruise Line. However, following financial problems she was sold to Fred Olsen in 1996, renamed **Black Watch** and entered service on 15 November that year. In February 1992 she suffered engine problems at Marmaris, Greece and was sent to Valletta to be repaired. She received a major overhaul at Blohm & Voss's yard at Hamburg in 2005 when her engines were replaced and the passenger space was refurbished.

The **Royal Daffodil** (488gt/62) was built as **Overchurch** for Birkenhead Corporation Ferries and conveyed Princess Alexandra at the opening of the new drydock at Cammell Laird's shipyard at Birkenhead in 1962. A ferry service was offered during the International Garden Festival in 1984 when the ferries were given a new livery of red, white and blue. **Overchurch** became the standby vessel in the early 1990s and was given a major refit in 1998. She was re-engined and returned to service the following year as **Royal Daffodil**. It was announced that **Royal Daffodil** was to undertake cruises to Llandudno during the summer months but this service never actually started, although she did carry out trials at the North Wales resort. It was an early morning departure from Langton lock by **Royal Daffodil** as she heads down the river to take up the ferry service at Seacombe. She is owned by Mersey Ferries. In October 2012 Merseytravel announced that the **Royal Daffodil** would be sold the following year. They later said that they were considering various options, which included loaning the vessel to a local museum or trust, with an option to be re-activated if required. She is now laid up in the East Float at Birkenhead.

The **Snowdrop** (464gt/60) was built by Philip & Son, Dartmouth, as **Woodchurch** for Birkenhead Corporation Ferries and entered service with her sister **Mountwood**. Both vessels were designed by the naval architects Graham and Woolnough to carry 1,200 passengers on the ferry service across the river. **Woodchurch** was laid up in 1980 but was back in service in 1983. Together with **Mountwood**, she received an extensive refit in 1989, returning the following year. The two sisters received a major overhaul and rebuilding in 2004, when **Woodchurch** was fitted with a new superstructure and funnel. She became **Snowdrop** in 2004 thus reviving a name carried by one of the Wallasey ferries over a century earlier. Each ferry is certified to carry a crew of six, which includes captain, mate, engineer, deck hands and two catering assistants. **Snowdrop** is owned by Mersey Ferries. She is seen berthed at the Seacombe Ferry Terminal.

Ben-my-Chree (IOM, 12747gt/98) was built at Van der Giessen-de Noord, Krimpen aan den IJssel, Rotterdam. She is owned by the Isle of Man Steam Packet Company. In Manx her name is translated "Girl of my heart". ***Ben-my-Chree*** was ordered in 1997 by Sea Containers for the Steam Packet as the company's first roll on/roll off vehicle ferry, and was built at a cost of £24 million. She was launched on 4 April 1998 as the sixth vessel of the same name to be built for the Steam Packet, and sailed on her maiden voyage on the Douglas to Heysham route on 5 July. During her 2004 overhaul at Birkenhead she was fitted with additional accommodation which increased her capacity from 500 to 636 passengers. She emerged from her 2008 overhaul with a new livery and a major internal refit. ***Ben-my-Chree*** is seen in the Crosby Channel.

The fast craft **Manannan** (IOM, 6360gt/98) was built at Incat Limited, Hobart, Tasmania in 1998 as **Incat 050** and was operated by Fast Cat Ferries in 1999 and 2000. She was then laid up at Hobart, becoming **USS Joint Venture** when she was chartered by the United States Government between 2001 and 2008, to enable them to evaluate the use of fast craft. She was purchased by the Isle of Man Steam Packet Company in 2008 and completed the voyage from Hobart to Portsmouth in 27 days where she was refitted by Burgess Marine. She arrived at Douglas, her home port on 11 May 2009, sailing on her maiden voyage to Liverpool on 22 May. She normally operates in the summer months and is usually laid up at Liverpool during the winter.

The **Hjaltland** (11486gt/02) was built at Aker Finnyards, Rauma and was owned by NorthLink Orkney & Shetland Ferries Ltd. The **Hjaltland** sails from the Mersey in May 2010 following the completion of her annual overhaul at Cammell Laird, Birkenhead. In 1999 the subsidised Northern Isles services were put out to tender. The routes were previously operated by P&O Scottish Services and the successful tender was awarded to a joint venture between the Royal Bank of Scotland and Caledonian MacBrayne. However, the contract was retendered and Caledonian MacBrayne formed NorthLink Ferries Limited, which commenced operations on 6 July 2006. NorthLink Ferries operated nightly sailings from Aberdeen to Lerwick, with four sailings a week via Kirkwall. The services are operated by **Hamnavoe**, **Hjaltland** and **Hrossey**, with two chartered freight vessels, **Hildasay** and **Helliar**. These vessels have continued in service after the Northern Isles routes were taken over by the Serco Group in July 2012.

The **Isle of Mull** (4719gt/88) was built at Appledore Ferguson Shipbuilders Ltd, Port Glasgow. She is owned by Caledonian Maritime Assets Ltd, CalMac Ferries Limited and we see her entering the drydock at Cammell Laird, Birkenhead. The **Isle of Mull** was lengthened by 5,4 metres by Tees Dockyard in 1988 because of a failure to meet the design criteria in terms of cargo capacity. The addition of the central section improved this capacity and seakeeping in addition to a slight increase in speed. She normally operates on the company's services between Oban and Craignure during summer and Oban and Colonsay in the winter months. Caledonian MacBrayne is the main operator of ferry services between the mainland of Scotland, and 22 of the major islands on the country's west coast. The company was renamed CalMac Ferries Limited in 2006 when it became a subsidiary of the holding company David MacBrayne Ltd which is owned by the Scottish government.

The cruise ferry *Oscar Wilde* (BHS, 31914gt/87) was built at the Wärtsilä shipyard in Turku. She is owned by Irish Ferries, Ireland. We see her arriving in the Mersey on 28 January 2011 for her annual overhaul by Cammell Laird at Birkenhead. She is normally employed on the company's Rosslare to Cherbourg and Rosslare to Roscoff routes. She was built as *Kronprins Harald* for the Jahre Line's Oslo-Kiel service. In 1991 her ownership was transferred to Color Line and she was sold to Irish Ferries in 2007, and chartered back to Color Line until September that year, when their new cruise ferry *Color Magic* was delivered. She was handed over to Irish Ferries on 2 September, renamed *Oscar Wilde* and entered service replacing *Normandy*. An engine room fire caused her to return to Falmouth on 2 February 2010 following her annual overhaul. There were no injuries and after repairs were completed she returned to service on 7 March when she sailed from Cherbourg to Rosslare.

The **Mersey Seaways** (27510gt/05) was built by Cantieri Navale Visentini at Porto Viro in Italy and entered service as **Mersey Viking**. Chartered by DFDS, she became **Mersey Seaways** in 2010. The **Mersey Seaways** and her sister **Lagan Seaways**, together with the Liverpool (Birkenhead) to Belfast route and two other vessels were sold to the Stena Line in 2011 in a deal costing £40 million. The two vessels offer both day and night sailings of approximately eight hours for the journey. **Mersey Seaways**, seen here off Gladstone Dock at the end of a voyage from Belfast, became **Stena Mersey** and **Lagan Seaways** was renamed **Stena Lagan**.

We now move on to dry cargo ships and we begin with container vessels. The Mediterranean Shipping Company was established in 1970 and began to handle containers towards the end of the 1970s. The company then grew rapidly thanks to the vision of its founder, Sorrento-based Gianluigi Aponte. His company bought wisely on the second-hand market and also chartered tonnage. The **MSC Rhone** (PAN, 36133gt/79) was built as **Hakuba Maru** at Mitsubishi Heavy Industries Limited, Kobe, Japan and was chartered by the Mediterranean Shipping Company, SA, Switzerland. She was renamed **Arcadian** in 2003 and became **MSC Rhone** in 2004. She was broken up at Alang in 2010. In this view she is being passed by the **Snaefell** off New Brighton in May 2009.

Many of the second-hand vessels bought by MSC came from well-established shipping companies in France, Germany and Japan. It was not until 1996 that newbuildings were acquired. As a general rule, the vessels owned by MSC have the names of people, usually female, associated with Aponte's family and colleagues, whilst chartered ships have geographical names. The **MSC Serena** (PAN, 39991gt/77), outward bound from Gladstone Dock, was built as **Stuttgart Express** at Flenderwerft, Lübeck, Germany. She is owned by the Mediterranean Shipping Company, SA, Switzerland. She was lengthened in 1985 and renamed **Maersk Algeciras** in 1992, **New York Express** in 1996, **Zim Eilat** in 1998 and **MSC Serena** in 2002. **MSC Serena** was broken up in 2009.

The **Ottowa Express** (BMU, 39174gt/98), outbound from Gladstone Dock, was built as **Canmar Honour** at Daewoo Shipbuilding & Marine Engineering Co Limited, Goeje, South Korea. This container ship was renamed **CP Honour** in 2005, CP Ships being a container shipping company and part of the Canadian Pacific Railway conglomerate. CP Ships was taken over by a large German company in 2005 and was allocated to that company's Hapag-Lloyd subsidiary. Thus the **CP Honour** became **Ottowa Express** in 2006. Hapag Lloyd have made Liverpool the sole United Kingdom port of call for their St Lawrence Coordinated Services (SLCS) serving Montreal and the line loads cargo at the Royal Seaforth Container Terminal. As we have already noted, the capacity at this terminal was expanded in 2012 with the addition of 5000 extra ground slots. This was achieved alongside the growth from an earlier £1.1 million investment in the ports IT systems with an upgrade to the TOS, a new wi-fi network, activation of a new Global Positioning System (GPS) for the port's straddle carriers and the introduction of an in-house designed SMART Vehicle Booking System.

The ***City of Glasgow*** (HKG, 14050gt/78), carrying a traditional Ellerman name, was built as ***Alltrans Express*** by Hitachi Shipbuilding Company, Mukaishima Onomichi, Japan, and became ***TFL Express*** and ***Nedlloyd Express*** in 1980, ***Express*** and ***Durga Osaka*** in 1986, ***Express*** again in 1988, ***Zim Guan*** in 1987, ***MSC Laura*** and ***Express*** in 1990, ***Choyang*** ***Express*** in 1993, ***Express*** and ***City of Glasgow*** in 1998. This series of names, many identifying the chartering company, is typical of many container vessels. At the time of the photograph, she was owned by Costamare Shipping Company SA and linked Liverpool and Dublin to Salerno. She was broken up in 2009.

The **Atlantic Concert** (SWE, 57255gt/84), seen in the Crosby channel, was built at the Kockum yard in Malmo, Sweden. She is owned by the Atlantic Container Line (ACL) which offers a weekly container and roll-on/roll-off service between North America and Europe. Atlantic Container Line was established in the late 1960s as a consortium of five major European shipping companies and is now owned by the Grimaldi group. ACL operate five similar vessels which were introduced in 1984-85 and each has an effective capacity of 3,100 TEUs. In 2011 **Atlantic Concert** transported the Orient Express antique Pullman dining carriage from Liverpool to Elizabeth, New Jersey. The carriage, weighing 43 tons was shipped on a low loader which was driven onto the vessel via her 420 metric ton capacity stern ramp. Following celebrations for the New York Stock Exchange marking the Orient Express Hotels Limited Independent Public Offering, the carriage was shipped back to Liverpool to resume operations with the Orient Express company's luxury fleet.

The **CSAV Renaico** (LBR, 35975gt/07), seen leaving Gladstone Dock, was built at the Shanghai Shipyard, Shanghai, China. She is owned by the Norddeutsche Reederei H Schuldt GmbH & Co, KG, Germany. This container ship was originally named **Northern Defender** but was delivered as **CSAV Renaico** after being chartered by Comapañia Sud Americana de Vapores (CSAV). This is a Chilean company founded in 1872 and the largest company of its kind in Latin America. Originally it offered only coastal services along the west coast of South America but the opening of the Panama Canal allowed rapid expansion and it soon offered services to the rest of the world. **CSAV Renaico** was renamed **Northern Defender** in 2013.

The **Independent Pursuit** (LBR, 15487gt/05), photographed in the Crosby channel in June 2007, was built at the Jiangsu Yangzijiang shipyard, Jiangyin City, China. She is owned by Peter Döhle Schiffahrts KG, Germany. This container ship was originally named **Heide** and became **Independent Pursuit** in 2006. The Independent Container Line started calling at Liverpool in October 1999, offering a container service from Antwerp and Liverpool to Chester (PA), and Wilmington (NC). The line's main markets are the north-east states of the USA but they do accept cargo for other parts of the United States. She was renamed **Calisto** in September 2010.

The *Gracechurch Star* (ATG, 8246gt/06), inbound in the Crosby channel, was built at the Detlef Hegemann Rolandwerf yard, Bremen, Germany. Launched as *Diana J* for Jungerhans Maritime Services, she became *Katherine Borchard* in 2006, *Gracechurch Star* in 2007, *BG Felixstowe* in 2009 and *Diana J* in 2010. Gracechurch Container Line was taken over by Borchard Line in 1989 but Borchard retained the former company name for some of its services and also for its road transport services.

The *Coastal Deniz* (ATG, 3125gt/91), photographed as she left Gladstone Dock, was built as *Sybille* by Krögerwerft GmbH, Rendsburg, Germany. She is owned by Sybille Reederei Ludtke KG, Germany. This coastal container vessel became *Baltic Bridge* and *Sybille* again in 1993, *Rhein Merchant* in 1995, *Sybille* in 2000 and *Coastal Deniz* in 2005. The Coastal Container Line is a subsidiary of the Mersey Docks and Harbour Company, itself owned by Peel Ports. The line operates a round trip service thrice weekly on both the Liverpool - Dublin and Liverpool - Belfast routes. At the time, the line was the Irish Sea's only lift-on/lift-off operator and it is able to provide specialist services for cargoes that are heavy, delicate, long or unusually shaped. *Coastal Deniz* is now operating a very successful container shuttle service between the Seaforth Container Terminal and Irlam on the Manchester Ship Canal.

From container ships, we move on to other dry cargo vessels. We see the **Stella Gemma** (LBR, 22402gt/09) off Fort Perch Rock at New Brighton. She was built as **Pretty Asia** at Nantong Chang Qing Sha Shipyard, Rugao, China. She is owned by United Tristan Da Cunha GmbH, Germany, and was renamed **Stella Gemma** in 2009. She became **United Tristan Da Cunha** in July 2012.

The **Soul of Luck** (PAN, 38716gt/91) was built at Shin Kurushima Onishi Shipyard, Imabari, Japan. She was owned by Soul of Luck Shipping Limited, Greece. This woodchips carrier was built as **Forest King** becoming **Soul of Luck** in 2009 and **Yildizlar** in 2011 when she was sold to Turkish owners for US$11 million. The sale was completed on 21 January at Semrang, Indonesia, prior to proceeding to Singapore for a crew change. We see her in the Crosby channel prior to berthing in the Royal Seaforth Dock in February 2009.

Also in the Crosby channel, the **Tai Kang Hai** (PRC, 22041gt/85) was built at Hudong Zhonghua Shipbuilding Company, Shanghai. She is owned by COSCO Bulk, Tianjin, China. COSCO was established in 1961 and now owns and controls over 800 modern vessels with a total tonnage of 56 million tonnes deadweight, and an annual carrying capacity of 400 million tons. The line's services cover over 1600 ports in more than 160 countries worldwide and its fleet size is the largest in China and second in the world. Its container fleet is the fifth in size in the world and the dry bulk fleet is the largest. COSCO also operate a large fleet of oil tankers and owns logistics facilities and resources. They are also involved in ship building and ship repairing, owning a total of 16 docks with large size ship and ocean engineering construction, refitting and repair. These facilities annually repair and refit over 500 large vessels and build up to 8.4 million tons. It owns more than 1000 companies and branches in over 50 countries and employs 130,000 people, of whom 400 are permanently stationed overseas and 4000 are foreign employees.

A visitor to Merseyside is sure to see the huge piles of scrap metal on the quaysides where once there used to be transit sheds. Some of the scrap is generated in north-west England and some is imported from other ports for re-export to the Far East, the Indian subcontinent and Turkey. Passing buoy C23 in the Crosby channel and no doubt inbound to load scrap for her home country, the *Halis Kalkavan* (TUR, 22629gt/84) was built by Hyundai Heavy Industries, Ulsan, South Korea. She is owned by Kalkavan Transport Denizcilik, Istanbul, Turkey. She was launched as *Esmeralda*, then became *Esmeralda 1* and was renamed *Halis Kalkavan* in 1995.

The **Jumbo Spirit** (NLD, 4962/95), passing the radar tower at Seaforth, was built at YVC Ysselwerf, Capelle aan den IJssel, Netherlands. She has one crane and one derrick, each capable of lifting 250 tonnes. Jumbo is one of the major heavy lift shipping lines and has recently developed interests in the offshore subsea installation market. The company operates a fleet of twelve specialised heavy lift vessels with a lifting capacity from 500 up to 1800 tons. The new vessels introduced from 2013 have a lifting capacity of 3000 tons. All the vessels in the fleet have a flush working deck, adjustable tween deck and some are allowed to sail with open hatches. They are designed with a shallow draught and a service speed of 17 knots. In April 2013 **Jumbo Spirit** finished sailing around the world transporting a mobile harbour crane and refinery equipment. The voyage started in Australia, then to New Zealand, the Bahamas and finished in Long Harbour, Canada.

The **CSE Harmony Express** (PAN, 39727gt/02) is inward bound in the Crosby channel and approaching Royal Seaforth Dock on 3 February 2009. She remained in port for eight days, eventually leaving for Belfast. The ship was built at Imabari Shipbuilding Company, Imabari, Japan. She is owned by the China Steel Express Corporation, Kaohsiung, Taiwan, part of the huge China Steel Corporation. With her seven hatches and an overall length of just under 225 metres, she is typical of the bulk carriers known as Panamax, so called because their dimensions allow them to transit the Panama Canal.

The Isle of Man Steam Packet vessel **Ben-my-Chree** passes the vehicle carrier **Asian Emperor** (PAN, 55729gt/99) as the latter prepares to swing in the river prior to docking at Gladstone Dock to unload her cargo in December 2008. The **Asian Emperor** was built at Hyundai, Ulsan, South Korea. She is owned by the International Shipholding Corporation of New Orleans and managed by LMS Ship management, Mobile. She has 12 car decks with a total car capacity of 6,402 vehicles. **Ben-my-Chree** is employed on the Douglas - Heysham service, but offers a service from the Isle of Man to the Twelve Quays Terminal, Birkenhead, at weekends during the winter months.

Our next type of vessel is the coastal dry cargo ship. The **Ben Varrey** (IOM, 997gt/86), passing through the dock system at Hornby Dock on 31 August 2011, was built at the Bodewes shipyard, Hoogezand, Netherlands. She is owned by the Ramsey Steamship Company Limited. Built as **Triumph**, she was renamed **Ben Varrey** in 1999. The Ramsey Steamship Company is a private limited company, incorporated in the Isle of Man which at the time of writing owned two coastal vessels that carried bulk cargoes in the Irish Sea and near Continent. Sadly, as we go to press, comes news that the company is possibly to cease trading because of an imminent demand for a huge sum of money as part of a contribution to an ailing pension fund.

The **Ben Ellan** (IOM, 538gt/81) was built by James W Cook & Company (Wivenhoe) Limited as **River Tamar** and was purchased by the Ramsey Steamship Company in 1990 when she was renamed **Ben Ellan**. The company was responsible for ship agency at all of the Manx ports and was also able to undertake engine overhauls, steel fabrication, welding work, and emergency repairs in its marine engineering department. It was a family-based firm which has operated for over 100 years serving the communities in the Irish Sea and around the Isle of Man. **Ben Ellan** was sold to Movada Pacific Incorporated, through Dick van der Kamp Shipsales BV, Netherlands on 20 October 2010. In 2012 she was sold again to Ali Mohamed-Hydar, Suriname. Her name was unchanged. In this view she is swinging in the River Mersey off Langton Dock.

The **Gina D** (507gt/75) was built as **Seaborne Trader** by the Yorkshire Dry Dock Company in Hull. She was owned by the Big Ditch Shipping Company. She became **Island Swift** in 1987, **Yeoman Rose** in 1990 and **Gina D** in 1999. She is normally employed carrying transhipped grain from Royal Seaforth Dock to Manchester. She and the vessel in the photograph below have returned to the trade for which they were built in the mid-1950s. At that time, they were operated by Bulk Cargo Handling Services, a division of the Alexandra Towing Company. Both vessels have been temporarily laid up awaiting a new berth after their previous berth was taken over for redevelopment. We see the **Gina D** on passage from the locks at Eastham to Langton Dock with Woodside ferry terminal in the background.

The **Trafford Enterprise** (507gt/74), seen soon after the locks at Eastham, was also built at the Yorkshire Dry Dock Company in Hull. She is owned by the Lincol-based Mainmast Logistics which took over the Big Ditch Company in December 2009. The company operates these two vessels which carry wheat from Liverpool to Manchester, where the cargo is then transferred to the nearby Rank Hovis flour mill in Trafford Park Road. It is estimated that each movement by sea saves 30 road truck movements, totalling 1100 miles. Mainmast was established in November 2001 operating motor tank barges dedicated to the edible oil industry on the River Hull and Humber, with a fleet capacity of 1200 tonnes between three tank barges. The company also provides stevedoring services for the discharge and loading of coastal vessels up to 3500 tonnes. The vessel operated as **Seacombe Trader** until 1998 when she was renamed **Sibir**, then **Elf** in 1999, **Calemax Enterprise** in 2005 and **Trafford Enterprise** in 2011.

The **CSL Clyde** (MLT, 4783gt/96), seen in the river off Egremont, was built as **Arklow Bridge** by Appledore Shipbuilders Ltd. She was launched on 4 November 1995 and completed on 3 January 1996. She has been owned by the CSL Group Inc (Canada Steamship Lines) since 2011 when she took her current name. She is a self-discharging vessel, which is employed carrying coal from Hunterston to Manisty Wharf near Ellesmere Port on the Manchester Ship Canal. The coal is destined for Fiddlers Ferry power station. Originally a conventional dry cargo ship she was converted for self-discharge in 2005 after purchase by Norwegian operators and renaming to **Clydenes** in 2005. In 2011 she was acquired by Canadian Steamship Lines and renamed **CSL Clyde**.

The **Red Duchess** (1285gt/69), inbound off Seaforth Dock, was built at Scheepswerf Hoogezand, Bergum, Netherlands. Launched as **Geertien Bos** and delivered as **Valdes**, she became **Bell Cavalier** (1973), **Valdes** (1974), **Bell Cavalier** (1975), **Minitrans** (1978), **Aasland** (1986) and **Red Duchess** in 2005. At the time of the photograph, she was owned by Troon-based Taylor and Taylor and was operated in the round timber trade by JST Services. This arrangement continued following her purchase by Coast Lines Shipping Ltd, an Irish company. She was sold in 2011 and at the time of writing is owned by a Dutch broker.

Sea conditions in the Mersey can be lively as this photograph proves. The **Wilson Saga** (CYP, 4200gt/98), ex **Borealnes**-88, requires assistance from the tug **Oakgarth** as she approaches the Alfred lock entrance. The ship was built by Brodgradiliste Apatin in Serbia and is part of the large Wilson Group fleet. Of special interest are the buildings of Waterloo Dock in the background. Designed by Jesse Hartley, the dock was opened in 1834 and was named after the Battle of Waterloo. In 1868 the dock was divided into two separate basins, East Waterloo and West Waterloo, and it was in East Waterloo Dock that corn warehouses were opened shortly afterwards. These were claimed to be the first grain warehouses in the world to handle bulk grain from a central power source which drove all elevators and conveyors. There were originally three blocks but the north block was destroyed during a bombing raid in 1941 and the south block was demolished in 1969 to allow the construction of a container terminal. The dock closed in 1988 and the east block was converted into residential apartments in 1990.

The **Arklow River** (NLD, 2999gt/03) was built at the Barkmeijer shipyard in Stroobos, Netherlands. She is owned by Arklow Shipping Limited which was formed in 1966 by Captains James Tyrrell and Victor Hall who wished to combine their small Arklow-based fleets to achieve greater efficiency. The fleet currently stands at 38 ships with a combined carrying capacity of 6 million tonnes annually. The vessels are singledeck, box hold and container fitted which are suited to the carriage of project cargoes, grain, general and bulk commodities. The **Arklow River**, seen off Seaforth Dock, became **Hagland Saga** in February 2011 after purchase by Norwegian owners.

The **Phantom** (GIB, 2329gt/00) approaches the Alfred Dock entrance at Birkenhead. Built by Peters Schiffswerf at Wewelsfleth in Germany, she is owned by Interscan Schiffahrts GmbH. This company was founded in 1973 and owns and charters multipurpose coasters for a wide variety of trades. It specialises, however, in the export of packaged timber from Scandinavia and the **Phantom** has a Finnish 1A ice classification enabling her to trade in difficult ice conditions.

In recent years, conventional coasters have been replaced by roll-on/roll-off vessels and we now look at some of these. The **Liverpool Viking** (21850gt/97), in the Crosby channel and heading for Dublin, was built at Cantieri Navale Visentini Porto Viro, Italy. She is owned by DFDS Seaways, Denmark. Norse Irish Ferries ordered two passenger and freight vessels from Visentini in 1996 and **Mersey Viking** and **Lagan Viking** were delivered for the Liverpool-Belfast route the following year. **Lagan Viking** sailed on her maiden voyage from Belfast on 16 November 1997, joining her younger sister which had started the new service in July that year. Initially, the ships used a berth within the dock system at Liverpool taking time to lock out into the river. However, the ships were transferred to the new river berth at Twelve Quays when this was opened in 2002. This allowed Norse Irish Ferries to provide two sailings a day on the route. In 2001 the ships were purchased by Norse Irish and transferred to the British register three years later. With the delivery of two larger vessels for the route, both ships were transferred to the Birkenhead-Dublin service in 2005. **Lagan Viking** became **Liverpool Viking** operated by Norfolk Line which had taken over the services. Following the sale of the line to DFDS, **Liverpool Viking** was renamed **Liverpool Seaways** in 2010. However, early in 2011, DFDS announced the closure of the service and **Liverpool Seaways** was transferred to a route linking Karlshamn in Sweden to Klaipeda in Lithuania.

The **Maersk Importer** (13107gt/96), in the Mersey estuary off the Bar lightship, was built at Miho Shipyard, Shizuoka, Japan. She was owned by Norfolk Line. **Maersk Importer** was employed on the Norfolk Line Irish Sea services from Heysham to Belfast and occasionally on their route from Birkenhead. She was transferred to the Irish Sea with two other vessels of the fleet in October 2009. They were bigger and faster than the vessels they replaced with **Maersk Importer** offering capacity for 120 trailers and a speed of 18 knots. Freight drivers were provided with a single en-suite cabin and meals cooked to order. The **Maersk Importer** was renamed **Hibernia Seaways** in 2010 and **Stena Hibernia** in August the following year. At the time of writing she trades between Travemünde in Germany and Helsingborg in Sweden.

This is a rare view of the *Clipper Pace* (CYP, 14759gt/09) off the Pier Head. Usually she berths directly at Langton dock but on this occasion she sailed upriver and turned off the Pier Head prior to entering the dock system. She was built by Astilleros de Huelva SA, Huelva, Spain and is owned by Seatruck Ferries Shipholding Limited. The *Clipper Pace* is the third of four new ships for the Seatruck Irish Sea fleet and entered service on the Liverpool-Dublin route in March 2009. Their service speed of over 21 knots enable the crossing time to be reduced and with the acquisition of the new vessels, Seatruck were able to employ their smaller vessels in the charter market. The four vessels are designed as the maximum size that can be accommodated at Heysham and have three decks for carrying vehicles. They carry up to 116 trailers, with accommodation for 12 passengers and 23 crew. Two sailings a day are offered by Seatruck Ferries on the Liverpool-Dublin route. The *Clipper Pace* was renamed *Seatruck Pace* in early 2012.

The **Clipper Point** (CYP, 14759gt/08), in Alfred Dock at Birkenhead, was also built by Astilleros de Huelva SA and was the first of the four new ships delivered in 2008/9. Seatruck operate three routes on the Irish Sea. They provide services between Liverpool-Dublin, Heysham-Warrenpoint and Heysham-Dublin. In 1997 they purchased the chartered **Riverdance** and the following year they added her sistership **Moondance** to their fleet.

Readers may recall that the **Riverdance** had to be broken up on the beach after being blown ashore north of Blackpool during bad weather on 31 January 2008 In 2003 Seatruck carried over 56,000 freight units, mainly unaccompanied trailers. In 2005 orders were placed for five new vessels and, in September 2007 they took over Celtic Link's Dublin-Liverpool route.

The **Seatruck Progress** (19722gt/11), leaving Langton lock for Dublin, is the first of a class of four vessels built at Flensburger shipyard. She is owned by Seatruck Ferries Shipholding Limited. Seatruck Ferries unaccompanied trailer operation on the Irish Sea rose by 58% in 2011 to over 300,000 units and the company now offer 80 sailings weekly from Liverpool-Dublin, Heysham-Dublin, Heysham-Warrenport and Heysham-Larne. However, the Heysham-Larne route was to be transferred to a new service from Liverpool-Belfast, but it did not materialise and the ships were chartered to Stena Line for their Irish Sea services. **Seatruck Performance** became **Stena Performer** and **Seatruck Precision** became **Stena Precision**. **Seatruck Progress** was awarded HANSA magazine's "Ship of the Year 2011" as the class is more efficient, less fuel consuming and more economic than comparative ships. The builders claim that, "the fuel consumption of the four ferries is up to 30% lower than conventional designs."

The **Merchant Bravery** (JAM, 5309gt/78), seen here in Alfred Dock, was built at Nylands Verksted, Oslo, Norway. She was launched as **Stevi** for Steineger & Wilk and was chartered to Norient Line and named **Norwegian Crusader**. In 1980 she was chartered to Ignazio Messina, becoming **Jolly Giallo**. When released from the charter in 1982 she was renamed **Norwegian Crusader** but was purchased by Ignazio Messina and named **Jolly Giallo** again. She was purchased by Merchant Ferries in 1993 and renamed **Merchant Bravery** operating on the Heysham -

Warrenpoint and later their Heysham - Dublin service. In 1999 she was operating on the Heysham - Belfast service for Belfast Freight Ferries and was transferred to the Heysham - Dublin service in 2004. She was sold in 2008, becoming **West Express** for Express Shipping A/S, and is now operating as **Ulfat** for Medmoryak Denizcilik of Istanbul, Turkey. Prior to entering service as **Ulfat** she was sent to the Sefine shipyard in Turkey, where she was converted to carry rail vehicles.

We now look at tankers and we begin with those importing crude oil to Tranmere Oil Terminal. The **BW Lake** (HKG, 158557gt/04), in the river off Trafalgar Dock, was built at Daewoo Shipbuilding & Marine Engineering, Goeje, South Korea. She is owned by the BW Shipping Group, Norway. World-Wide Shipping acquired Bergesen ASA in 2003 and, following a restructuring the company became the BW Group in 2005. It now comprises BW Gas, BW Offshore, BW Maritime, BW Ventures and BW Fleet Management, incorporated in Bermuda. The Group operates a fleet of 93 owned, part-owned or controlled ships specialising in tankers, liquefied natural gas carriers, liquefied petroleum gas carriers and offshore floating production vessels. The BW Group now employs around 300 people in the BW Gas and BW Offshore businesses in Oslo and 120 people at the BW Maritime office in Singapore, who are supported by a global network of representatives and agency offices with a total staff, including seafarers of over 4000 people.

The Malaysian crude oil tanker **Bunga Kasturi Empat** (MYS, 156967gt/07) was built at Universal Ariake Shipyard, Kumamoto, Japan. She is owned by the Malaysia International Shipping Corporation Berhad and is registered in Port Klang. She has nine watertight compartments and the cargo is carried in seventeen. Early in 2012 MISC announced that they would be withdrawing from the container ship business as they had lost $789 million over the previous three years. They would place its 16 containerships up for sale and concentrate on the intra-Asia trade and their fleet of crude oil tankers. We see her arriving in the River Mersey in September 2009, prior to docking at the Tranmere Oil Terminal at Birkenhead. From Tranmere, the crude oil is taken by pipeline to the oil refinery at Stanlow owned by Shell until 2011 but now owned by Essar, an Indian oil company.

The tanker **Energy Centaur** (IOM, 42298gt/08) was built at Sungdong Shipbuilding & Marine Engineering Company, Tongyoung, South Korea. She is part of the fleet of Enterprises Shipping & Trading SA, Greece, which was established in 1973 and manages a fleet of ocean-going reefer, bulk and container vessels which are chartered out for fixed periods of time. The company currently manages a fleet of 86 vessels, with six vessels under construction. Enterprise Shipping & Trading also provide technical and crew management, insurance and risk management, procurement, consultancy and the sale and purchase of vessels. Over 11 million tonnes of crude oil are imported through the port via the Tranmere Oil Terminal. The tankers discharge their cargo at a rate up to 10,000 tonnes an hour. The Stanlow refinery produces petrol and diesel, jet fuel, fuel oil, bunkers, LPG, specialist chemicals, base oil and lubricants. We see her in the channel at Crosby in June 2009.

The **Stolt Kestrel** (CYM, 3853gt/92), built by the Fukuoka Shipbuilding, in Japan, approaches the Alfred lock entrance. She is owned by Stolt-Nielsen SA, Norway. Stolt Tankers operate one of the world's largest fleet of deep-sea, regional, coastal and inland parcel tankers, providing transportation services to manufacturers of chemicals and other bulk liquids. The fleet is equipped with handling equipment, including heating and cooling systems, specialised cleaning equipment and nitrogen generators. Stolt-Nielsen are able to handle virtually any liquid cargo, including speciality chemicals, petrochemicals, commodity chemicals, oleo chemicals, vegetable oils, clean petroleum products, lubricating oils and acids.

The **Stolt Sandpiper** (3327gt/11) was built at Chongqing Chuandong Shipyard, Fuling, China. She is owned by Stolt-Nielsen SA. The Inter Europe Division provides services to north-west Europe, the east and west coast UK, German North Sea and southern Scandinavia, Bay of Biscay, the Iberian peninsula and the Mediterranean. The fleet consists of 20 fully stainless steel, double-hull chemical tankers with cargo capacities ranging from 4,200 dwt to 8,200 dwt. The **Stolt Pelican** (3711gt/96) was built as **Multitank Saxonia** at the Baltic Shipyard, St Petersburg, Russia. She is another vessel in the Stolt-Nielsen fleet. She carried her original name for only a year, her final voyage as such being from the River Tees to Swansea. She was then renamed **Isebek** and retained this name until entering the Stolt-Nielsen fleet in 2008. The vessels are passing near the Tranmere Oil Terminal.

The **Chartsman** (LBR, 4842gt/93), seen off Crosby, was the second of two tankers ordered by Rowbotham Tankships from the Malaysia Shipyard and Engineering Company in Johore. Not only was this a surprising choice of builder but even more surprising was the announcement that the ships would be registered in Liberia, the first vessels not to fly the Red Ensign in the history of this long-established British company. By the time they were delivered, ownership had been transferred to investment partnerships in Germany. In early 1993, P&O took full control of Rowbotham Tankships and then on 30 December 1996, P&O Tankships was sold to James Fisher & Sons plc. **Chartsman** was sold to Destiny Marine & Shipping Co Ltd in 2012 and was renamed **Masters Force II** under the Liberian flag.

The ***Bro Atland*** (DNK, 11377gt/99) was built at Factorias Vulcano, Vigo, Spain. She was launched as ***United Albert*** but entered service as ***United Atland*** in the summer of 1999. She was renamed ***Bro Atland*** in early October 2000. The story of the Broström group is complex. Axel Broström founded a shipping company in Gothenburg in 1890. After many years of prosperity, the several lines acquired by the Broström family suffered a decline in the 1970s and 1980s. In 1992, Broström Rederi AB was bought by United Tankers, a consortium of three Swedish tanker operators. It was this company that ordered the ***United Albert*** /***United Atland***. However, the Broström name was retained and indeed flourished in the late 1990s, hence the renaming of this tanker to ***Bro Atland*** which we see entering the River Mersey.

In modern times, the owning and operation of ships has become an increasingly complex matter. Not only do owning companies merge and pool resources but so do operators and commercial managers. Registers tell us that the *Cape Dawson* (8278gt/09) is owned by Mpc Munchmeyer Petersen Steamship Company, Hamburg, Germany. She traded in a consortium known as United Chemical Tankers (UCT) which was set up jointly by German owners Christian Ahrenkiel and Knöhr & Burchard. A Norwegian tanker operator, Bergen-based Seatrans, was also involved in this consortium. When the consortium was dissolved, the *Cape Dawson* was moved to United Product Tankers (UPT), another Ahrekiel offshoot, which explains the letters on the tanker's hull. She is seen in the River Mersey off Seacombe.

Finally in this tanker section, we look at a liquefied gas tanker. Lauritzen Kosan tankers was formed in mid-1989 when the huge Danish Lauritzen Group took over Kosan Tankers. The new company soon ordered four gas tankers from the Hermann Sürken shipyard in Papenburg. The first of these was the **Laura Kosan**, launched on 10 April 1992 and delivered on 28 July. All four were built to serve Guernsey Gas, a long established customer of Kosan. In 2006, Eitzen Gas took over some of the vessels in the Lauritzen Kosan Tanker fleet including the **Laura Kosan** which was renamed **Sigas Laura**. The tankers were painted initially in a joint Eitzen/Kosan livery but by the date of this photograph, taken off Crosby, all were in full Eitzen livery. She became **B Gas Laura** in October, 2011.

We now look at naval and auxiliary vessels. Photographed in the channel off Crosby, **HMS Illustrious** was built at Swan Hunter, Tyneside. She is the second of three *Invincible* class aircraft carriers and is the last carrier to be converted to operate helicopters following the retirement of the Harrier aircraft. She was ordered in May 1976 and was launched by Her Royal Highness, The Princess Margaret, Countess of Snowdon, on 14 December 1978. **HMS Illustrious** was commissioned on 20 June 1982, is based at Portsmouth and identified by her pennant number R06. She was converted to a commando and helicopter carrier during her £40 million refit in July 2011.

HMS Sutherland enters the river at New Brighton. She was the thirteenth of sixteen Type 23 frigates to be delivered and is the Royal Navy's fastest frigate, reaching more than 34 knots on trials in 2004. She was launched in 1996 at Yarrow's yard on the Clyde with a bottle of whisky, not champagne. She was the first warship to pass under the Skye Bridge, the first circumnavigation of the globe by a Royal Navy ship in fourteen years, and the first to receive and fire the updated Seawolf air defence missile system. She escorted **HMS Ocean** and **HMS Albion** to the Mediterranean in 2011 as part of the Response Force Task Group and saw action off the coast of Libya in support of the NATO OP Unified Protector. On 18 October 2011 she passed through Tower Bridge and berthed alongside to **HMS Belfast** for a five-day visit. In December 2012, she returned from a six-month deployment in the Indian Ocean and the Middle East and was placed in a period of maintenance. She returned to sea in 2013, participating in exercises with coalition forces such as Joint Warrior off the coast of Scotland and a visit to the county of Sutherland.

The **Orangeleaf** (18854gt/79) was built as **Hudson Progress** by Cammell Laird in Birkenhead and, in the same year of 1979, she became **Balder London**. She saw action in the Falkland Islands in 1982 while carrying fuel from Ascension. She was acquired by the Royal Fleet Auxiliary and was renamed **Orangeleaf** (A110) in 1984, following a major conversion which involved the installation of new navigation and communication electronics, fitting two replenishment rigs and extending the crew accommodation. In mid-2004 she took part in a deployment with the French carrier battle group and the aircraft carrier **Charles De Gaulle** (R91) in the Indian Ocean. Preparing to move through the dock system at Birkenhead, she shares the Alfred Dock basin with the **Stolt Shearwater** (CYM, 3811gt/98), built at the Affine shipyard in La Spezia.

The **Sir Bedivere** (7894gt/67), seen off Seacombe, was built by Hawthorn Leslie & Company, South Tyneside. On completion she was based at Marchwood, Hampshire, and saw service in the Falkland Islands in 1982 where she suffered slight damage whilst lying in San Carlos Water when a bomb glanced off the ship. On 16 November 1982 she returned to the UK repatriating 64 service personnel who had lost their lives in the campaign. In 1991 **Sir Bedivere** was deployed in the Persian Gulf and in 1994 she undertook an extensive overhaul when she was lengthened by 12 metres. She was operating in Sierra Leone in 2000 and became the command vessel for British and American ships in 2003 during Operation Telic. In 2002 she was operating in the Persian Gulf with four British minesweepers and then as a troop support vessel for the Royal Marines. Following a successful operation she returned to Britain the following year with the boats and men of 539 Assault Squadron Royal Marines. She was decommissioned on 18 February 2008 and was sold to the Brazilian Navy becoming **NDCC Almirante Saboia**.

The next four pages look at ships being overhauled and/or repaired. The **Bibby Sapphire** (MLT, 6064gt/05) was built as **Volstad Surveyor** at the Celik Tekne Shipyard, Istanbul, Turkey. She was acquired by Bibby Ship Management Ltd in 2002, becoming **Bibby Sapphire**. She is a DP Class 2 offshore support vessel which is designed to operate in severe weather conditions. She has compensated cranes, 300 metre depth rated saturation diving systems, permanently installed ROVs and spacious deck areas and accommodation. Bibby Offshore Limited opened an office in Aberdeen in 2003 and was established as a separate division of the Bibby Line Group in 2007. Cammell Laird & Company completed a refit on **Bibby Sapphire** at Birkenhead in 2006.

The **Seniority** (3860gt/06), also in the Cammell Laird drydock, was built at Qingshan Shipyard, Wuhan, China. She is owned by James Fisher Shipping Services. F T Everard operated coastal cargo services for over 100 years and by the 1960s they owned one of the largest fleets in Europe. By 2006 the fleet comprised eleven tankers, nine of which they owned, with four tankers due to enter service the following year. They also owned Cattledown Wharf on the River Plym at Plymouth. In December that year the company was acquired by James Fisher & Sons which enabled them to operate a predominately modern double-hulled fleet, to accelerate the expansion of its other divisions and to refinance Everard's ships. The James Fisher Group anticipated that the acquisition would enable the cash flow benefits from an enlarged and integrated tankship fleet to pursue further expansion in the company's other divisions. The main growth in the fleet in recent years has been in marine support services, comprising offshore oil, specialist technical and defence divisions.

The Cammell Laird drydock is occupied on this occasion by the *European Highlander* (BHS, 21188gt/02), built by MHI Shimonoseki Shipyard & Machinery Works in Japan. She is employed on P&O's Irish Sea services from Larne to Cairnyan and is slightly longer than her sister, *European Causeway*, which is employed on the same service. She was built at a cost of £35 million and is designed to carry 410 passengers, 375 vehicles on her 1825 lane metres. In January 2005, she grounded while attempting to berth at Cairnryan in heavy winds. She was successfully refloated the following day and no injuries or pollution resulted from the accident. The Chief Inspector of the Marine Accident Investigation Branch supported the actions that the crew had taken and recommended that, in future, the radar should be properly adjusted and set to an appropriate range scale. The Olympic Flame was carried on board from Northern Ireland to Scotland on 7 June 2012.

Our final drydock view shows the **Stena Europe** (24828gt/81), built as **Kronprinsessan Victoria** at Götaverken Cityvarvet in Gothenburg. She is owned by Stena Line AB. Operating on Stena's Fishguard to Rosslare route **Stena Europe** occasionally visited the Mersey for her annual overhaul at Cammell Laird's shipyard at Birkenhead. As **Kronprinsessan Victoria**, she worked on the Gothenburg-Frederikshavn and then Gothenburg - Kiel routes. She was renamed **Stena Saga** when transferred to the Oslo - Frederikshavn route in 1988. Six years later, a move to the Harwich - Hook of Holland route saw her become **Stena Europe** and then **Lion Europe** in 1997 after moving to the Karlskrona - Gdynia route of Lion Ferries, a subsidiary of Stena Line. She reverted to **Stena Europe** the following year when all of the Lion Ferries services were branded under the Stena banner. After a major refit at the yard which built her, she transferred to Stena's Fishguard - Rosslare route in Spring 2002.

The **Sand Swan** (1204gt/70) was built at J Bolson & Sons Limited, Poole. Latterly, she was owned by Mersey Sand Suppliers Limited. **Sand Swan** operated as a suction dredger on the River Mersey on most days and she is seen here working off New Brighton. She would unload her cargo of sand at her berth in the Liverpool dock system and returned to work the following day anchored in the river. In 2010 she was sold to owners in Klaipeda, Lithuania. Three years later, she remains in the Liverpool dock system, neglected and in steadily deteriorating condition.

The **Mersey Mariner** (2135gt/81) was built at the Robb Caledon shipyard in Leith for the Mersey Docks and Harbour Company, this company becoming a subsidiary of Peel Ports in September 2005. She was employed dredging the channels, dock system and the approach to the river entrances. When Peel Ports decided to contract this work to private dredging companies she was sold to Bandeirantes Dragagem & Construcao, Rio de Janeiro, Brazil in July 2009 and renamed **Mersey M**. We see her passing Langton Dock and leaving the river for the final time.

The **WD Mersey** (1595/84) was built as **Bragadin** by Lucchese Achille, Italy for the Ministry of Public Works branch of the Government of Italy. She was sold to the Westminster Dredging Company in mid-2008 and renamed **WD Mersey**. Westminster Dredging was an offshoot of Boskalis, a family owned company in the Netherlands. When this offshoot was registered in the 1930s, the Dutch owners wanted an impressive English name and so chose Westminster. This suction hopper dredger operates on the Manchester Ship Canal, the Mersey approaches and various smaller ports in the Irish Sea. **WD Mersey** has a hopper capacity of 1826m^3 and is able to dredge to a depth of 28 metres with one section pipe of a diameter of 0.7 metres. Her discharge system consists of the bottom doors opening or the cargo is pumped ashore.

The **WD Medway II** (CYP, 3122gt/76) was built as **WD Medway** at the Verolme shipyard in Heusden, Netherlands. She was owned by Westminster Dredging Company Limited and was lengthened and converted from a grab hopper dredger to trailing suction dredger in 1988. She was renamed **WD Medway II** in that same year. She originally had a hopper volume of 1521m^3 but this increased to 3600m^3 after her conversion. She operated at a dredging depth of 25 metres, which could be extended to 40 metres with a suction pipe of 0.8m. **WD Medway II** was broken up in 2010.

The **Crestway** (CYP, 5005gt/08) was built at the IHC Merwede BV yard in Kinderdijk in the Netherlands. She is owned by Boskalis Westminster, NV, Netherlands. **Crestway** is the second of two medium sized 5.600 m³ trailing suction hopper dredgers built for Boskalis. **Shoreway** and **Crestway** were ordered to be used in the global Boskalis dredging operations, and have been specially designed for dredging and the transportation of sand and sludge. They also work in shallow waters for the maintenance of harbours, beach replenishment and land reclamation projects. Both vessels are equipped with the latest computer systems to control and optimise the dredging process. Three main engines have been installed, two are dedicated for propulsion and one for driving the dredge pump during trailing. During the discharge to shore, the two main engines drive the dredge pump and one main engine is used for propulsion. The **Crestway** is passing an outward bound Atlantic Container Line vessel off New Brighton.

The **UKD Orca** (2972gt/10), was built at the Barkmeijer shipyard in Stroobos in the Netherlands. She is owned by UK Dredging, established in 1996 as a division of Associated British Ports. **UKD Orca** was designed to undertake dredging and maintenance work in ports, rivers, sea channels and estuaries around the UK. She is fitted with a 700mm suction pipe suitable for dredging at depths of 25 metres. An electrically driven dredge pump in the pump room serves the port or starboard side suction pipe. The dredge pump is also used to empty the hopper via six suction openings in the bottom door recesses. She has been fitted with two electrically driven rudder propellers and a bow thruster. The main navigation and dredging console is housed in the wheelhouse to allow the operator a perfect view of the suction pipes and the hopper. The photograph shows her working in the River Mersey off Seaforth Dock on 10 June 2011.

Tugs are an essential part of the operation of any major port and it is those vessels we now look at. The **Oakgarth** (452gt/84) was built by McTay Marine at Bromborough on the south bank of the Mersey. She was launched on 22 October 1984 and delivered on 14 December. The McTay yard had built two similar tugs three years earlier, but the **Oakgarth** and later sister **Yewgarth** were more powerful and had firefighting monitors on top of the mainmast. After delivery, the tug was stationed in Cabinda on the west coast of Africa prior to returning to the UK. Also in the photograph are the **Ashgarth** which we see on the page opposite and the **Svitzer Stanlow**, a tug built to escort large tankers in the Mersey. The tugs are seen approaching the Langton lock entrance after completing towage duties on the river.

The **Ashgarth** (307gt/92), seen approaching the Alfred Dock entrance, was built as **Senho Maru** at the Kanagawa shipyard in Kobe in Japan. She was launched on 29 July 1992 and delivered to her Japanese owners on 25 September. In the late summer of 1998 she was purchased by Cory Towage Ltd and eventually arrived in the Mersey on 14 December 1998. She was refitted and modified but still retained her distinctively Japanese outline. In 2000, Cory Towage was bought by a large Dutch company, Wijsmuller. The ink had barely dried on the takeover documents, and likewise the paint on the tugs, before Wijsmuller itself was taken over by A P Møller, a huge Danish company, which henceforth operated the tugs through Em Z Svitzer, a Møller subsidiary.

Newly-built Svitzer tugs have been given Svitzer names followed by a suffix meant to reflect the tug's area of operation. As tugs are frequently moved from one area to another, such a naming scheme soon became futile. The **Svitzer Maltby** (385gt/05) was built at AB Baltijos Laivu Statykla, Klaipeda, and completed at Lindø in Denmark. She is owned by Svitzer Marine Limited. **Svitzer Maltby** was part of an order of ten tugs of the same type built in Lithuania for Svitzer fleets around Britain, Europe and Scandinvia. **Svitzer Mallaig**, **Svitzer Mull** and **Svitzer Maltby** were delivered to operate around Britain and have Caterpillar 3516 diesels delivering 5842bhp at 1600rev/min for a bollard pull of 70 tonnes towing ahead, 65 tonnes astern and a maximum speed of 14 knots.

The second half of the twentieth century saw a continuous process of takeovers and mergers throughout the shipping industry. Towage was not exempt. The Alexandra Towing Company Limited had, by 1990, become one of the two main towage companies on the Mersey. In 1992, Alexandra was sold to Howard Smith Towing, an Australian company rapidly expanding into the UK. In 2001, Howard Smith was sold to another Australian company, Adsteam. Five years later, Svitzer wished to takeover Adsteam and that proposal raised serious issues about competition as it already owned the former Cory Towage. It was decided that Svitzer would have to sell the Adsteam operation on the Mersey and this was bought by Dutch towing company Smit. The hull of the **Smit Donau** (289gt/07), in the river off Egremont, was built at Gdynia and the tug was completed at the Damen shipyard in Gorinchem. She was intended for the Smit fleet in Rotterdam but was immediately transferred to the Mersey fleet where she arrived in the early hours of 2 June 2007.

The **Smit Sandon** (398gt/96) was built by Astilleros Armon at Navia in northern Spain. She is owned by Smit Harbour Towage. **Smit Sandon** is a sea-going Voith Schneider tug with a bollard pull of 41 tonnes ahead, and was launched as **Schelde 20**, operating for the Scheldt Towing Company at Antwerp. She was renamed **Smit Sandon** in August 2009 when she arrived on the River Mersey. We see her off Tranmere Oil Terminal with the Stanlow oil refinery in the far distance.

For a Mersey tug, the **Smit Gladstone**, seen in the river off the Pier Head, had a relatively unusual history. She was launched at the Jadewerft yard in Wilhelmshaven on 27 November 1976 and delivered to Hapag-Lloyd on 4 January 1977. She served this German company as **Herkules** until 1990 when she was chartered to Alexandra Towing and, retaining her orange Hapag-Lloyd hull, was renamed **TS Herkules**. The charter was transferred to Howard Smith and then to Adsteam, the latter company changing her name to **Gladstone** in 1994. When taken over by Smit in 2007, she was renamed **Smit Gladstone** but her stay on the Mersey was brief. In mid-November, she was sold to Iskes Towage & Salvage, of IJmuiden, and renamed **Hercules**.

The **Anglian Monarch** (1485gt/99), photogaphed passing Seaforth Dock, was built by Matsuura Iron Shipbuilding, Osakikamijima, Japan for Klyne Towage and was one of four vessels contracted to the UK's Maritime and Coastguard Agency to patrol approximately 33,000 square miles of British waters. They were stationed in the Dover Straits, the South-West Approaches, the Hebrides and the Northern Isles with the **Anglian Monarch** usually working in the Dover Straits. All four vessels were equipped with extensive towing equipment to enable them to offer a wide range of emergency services. The vessels played a major role in salvage work, fire-fighting, flood control, casualty evacuation, search and rescue,

pollution counter measures, recovery of floating debris, anchor-handling, vessel escort and hydro graphic surveying. In 2007, J P Knight acquired Klyne Towage and three years later the UK government announced that it would end the contract to provide emergency towing vessels. The **Anglian Monarch** is laid up at Invergordon and offered for sale at the time of writing. The Scottish subsidiary J P Knight (Caledonian) Limited operates a modern fleet of tugs engaged in a wide variety of towage and support activities, shiphandling, coastal and deep-sea contract towage, and offshore support operations.

The **Vos Pathfinder** (1433gt/08) passes the inbound **Atlantic Cartier** off Gladstone Dock. She was built at the Astilleros Zamakona shipyard in Bilbao in Spain and is owned by Vroon Offshore Services Limited. Vroon has been operating offshore services for over 40 years in the North Sea, Mediterranean and South East Asia, with offices in Aberdeen, Den Helder, Genoa and Singapore. They have a fleet of Platform Supply Vessels (PSV), Anchor Handling Tugs (AHTS) vessels, emergency response and rescue vessels (ERRV) and subsea support vessels. Also, they offer a wide range of additional offshore services which are provided on a worldwide basis, such as seismic/survey support, maintenance and scientific support. They operate in the fields of oil drilling and production along with offshore construction and maintenance work.

The **Vos Ocean** (BRB, 753gt/83) was built at the McDermott shipyard in New Iberia in Louisiana. She is also owned by Vroon Offshore Services Limited. It operates over 100 vessels. Over 50 new vessels have been added to the fleet since 2007 and older units have been sold or broken up. The company is still privately held by the Vroon family and is managed by its fourth generation. It was founded in 1890 to export agricultural products from the Netherlands to England, France and Belgium while importing coal.

With ample wharfage available, the docks in Liverpool and Birkenhead are often used to lay up vessels. In the summer of 2009, four coastal tankers were laid up in Vittoria Dock, Birkenhead, all from the James Fisher Everard fleet. From left to right, we see the **Sarnia Liberty** (GIB, 3017gt/08), ex **Vedrey Thor**-09; **Asperity** (2965gt/97); **Seniority** and **Superiority** (both BHS, 3859gt/06). The **Sarnia Liberty** had recently been bought by the States of Guernsey and was waiting to enter service with Fisher Everard as managers. It was stated at the time that the other three tankers were being offered for sale but all of them subsequently returned to trade in the Fisher Everard fleet.

The **Most Sky** (PAN, 1972gt/06) was built by the Zhejiang Hongxin Shipbuilding Company, Taizhou Zhejiang, China. She was detained at Birkenhead in 2010 by the Marine and Coastguard Agency (MCA) over concerns about the conditions on board and the fact that the Turkish, Azerbaijani and Georgian crew had not been paid any wages. The International Transport Workers Federation, local people and companies provided assistance and food for the crew, who later received money and tickets to return home. The MCA described the engine room as the worst they had seen and there was no fresh fruit or vegetables on board and no heating. The **Most Sky** became **Prodromos** in July, 2012 and she is owned by Dekathlon Marine SA, Salamina, Greece. Although repainted and looking respectable, she remains in the West Float at Birkenhead at the time of writing in mid-2013.

The final section of our book looks at a miscellaneous group of ships. Seen berthed in Canning Dock, the *Fitzcarraldo* (286gt/71) was built as the *Bjarkøy* by Nord Offshore, Sandnessjoen, Norway, and operated on passenger and cargo services around Tromsø in Norway. She was purchased by the Walk The Plank Company in 1992 and used as a theatre ship, touring British ports and harbours in Scotland, Ireland, England and Wales. Her hold was converted into a theatre where 125 people could sit on the aft deck to watch the performances. Audiences also sat on the quayside for some productions and later moved to the ship's hold as the story continued. WTP Pyrotechnics who create fire shows, firework displays and outdoor spectacles, donated all their profits to the Walk The Plank Company. This was a major source of income for the company, together with arts grants and donations. However, rising costs forced the company to sell the ship and she sailed from the River Mersey at the end of May 2010 to a new home in the Netherlands as a floating nightclub.

The ***Fugro Saltire*** (9603gt/08) was built at the Gdansk Shipyard in Poland. She is owned by Forland Shipping AS, Norway. Fugro is a technical consultancy providing subsea surveying and data interpretation services for the oil and gas industry. It provides remotely operated vehicle support vessel services for vessels, mobile offshore drilling units and its own vessels. A contract was signed by them in May 2006 for the long-term charter of the ***Fugro Saltire*** to provide offshore construction and subsea support, alongside the company's remotely controlled vehicles. The vessel provides support, inspection, repair and maintenance services and Fugro has an option to purchase the vessel after 2013. ***Fugro Saltire*** has a helideck designed for a Sikorsky S61/S92 helicopter with a maximum load of 12,800kg. It has a moon pool, which is used for module handling, and features under deck chemical tanks to provide storage and discharge capability for pipeline commissioning chemicals. The ship has cabin space for 105 crew and the facilities on board include a gymnasium, conference rooms, an internet café and full air conditioning. She is seen here leaving Langton Dock after a crew change on 9 March 2011.

The **MPI Resolution** (14310gt/03), photographed in the Crosby channel, was built as **Mayflower Resolution** at the Shanhaiguan shipyard in Qinhuangdao, China and is a wind turbine installation vessel. Claimed to be the first of her kind, she cost £53 million. She has been used in various locations around the UK including the Barrow Offshore Wind Farm and the Robin Rigg Wind Farm off the Cumbrian coast. By lowering her six legs on to the seabed, the vessel can raise herself between 3 metres and 46 metres above sea level and she is able to work in water to a depth of 35 metres. The search for oil and gas in the Irish Sea and more recently the construction of wind farms have brought a wide variety of specialised vessels to the River Mersey and this vessel is certainly specialised. She became **Resolution** in 2004 and **MPI Resolution** in 2009.

The **Bibby Tethra** (234gt/11) was built by Socarenam, Boulogne, France. She is owned by Bibby Maritime Limited. **Bibby Tethra** is a purpose-built semi-swath hydrographic coastal survey vessel, which is equipped for a team of sixteen personnel with eight cabins, lounge and kitchen. She is chartered by "Osiris Projects", who are responsible for seabed mapping and geophysical surveys, oceanography, ordnance detection and object location, maritime archaeology and other environmental monitoring projects. The company was established in 1997 and is based in the Wirral. They have conducted over 350 marine-based contracts throughout the UK and northern Europe involving offshore wind farms, tidal power and wave energy developments. **Bibby Tethra** began her working life conducting inspections of oil and gas pipelines in the Irish Sea and is seen in the River Mersey on 21 May 2011.

Now an accommodation vessel, the **Wind Ambition** (13336gt/74) leaves Gladstone Dock to take up position at a wind farm in the Irish Sea. She was built at the Wärtsilä shipyard in Turku as the passenger and vehicle ferry **Prinsessan Birgitta** for the Sessan Line and was operated by Stena Line in 1981-82, retaining the same name. However, Stena renamed her **Stena Scandinavica** in 1982 and she became **Scandinavica** in 1989 with a brief charter to CoTuNav (Tunisian Ferries) seeing her renamed **Tarek L** in that same year before reverting to **Scandinavica**. Between 1990 and 1994 she was placed on Color Line's service as **Venus** and was operating as **King of Scandinavia** for DFDS Seaways from 1994-2001. She returned again to Tunisia Ferries as **King of Scandinavia** in 2001 and was also operating for Bornholmstrafikken that year. A charter to NATO followed in 2002 and she became **Cesme** for Marmara Lines from 2002 to 2010. She was purchased and refitted by C-bed Floating Hotels of Schipol in the Netherlands in 2010 and was christened **Wind Ambition** on 23 July at a ceremony in Fredericia, Denmark. She has been based at Liverpool during her work at the Walney wind farm project in the Irish Sea in 2012.

The **Aestus**, seen in the East Float at Birkenhead, was constructed by James & Stone Limited at Brightlingsea in 1981. She is a river survey boat and was built to work on the River Mersey for the Mersey Docks & Harbour Company. She is powered by two Deutz BA 6M 816/LLK/U marine diesels, each 354bhp, at 1800rpm with twin disc MG514 reversing gearboxes. She was subsequently bought by Carmet Towage, owners of the ship handling tugs on the Manchester Ship Canal, and was then sold to Thames Towage for work on that river. Her mast has now been removed.

The **Galatea** (3672gt/07), seen working on the Brazil buoy off New Brighton, was built by Stocznia Remontowa SA, Gdansk, Poland. She is Trinity House's multi-functional tender which was delivered in 2007, and christened by Her Majesty The Queen on 17 October that year alongside **HMS Belfast**. **Galatea** was a replacement for the **Mermaid** and her delivery to Trinity House represented the final stage of a £38 million investment in three new vessels by the UK and Irish General Lighthouse Authorities. **Galatea** is a sistership to the **Pharos** which is in service with the Northern Lighthouse Board in Scotland. She incorporates DPAA dynamic positioning, a range of high specification survey equipment, a 30 ton lift crane, a moon pool, a large working deck with the facility to lock containers on deck with plug in to 230V or 400V supply, a helicopter landing pad and a high speed workboat.

The **Patricia** (2541gt/82), photographed off Gladstone Dock, was built by Henry Robb Limited, Leith. She is Trinity House's multi-functional tender and works around the coast of England, Wales and the Channel Islands on maintenance duties, towing, wreck location and other aids to navigation projects. **Patricia** is equipped with accommodation for twelve passengers, a helicopter landing pad, 20 tonne main crane, 28 tonne bollard pull and towing winch. She is responsible for maintaining, repairing and examining aids to navigation, research projects and the deployment and recovery of scientific equipment, marine hazard search and recovery, lifting, towing and positioning of marine equipment, sea trials of electronic equipment, helicopter support and guard duties for cable and pipe laying projects. It is possible for the general public to sail as passengers on the **Patricia**.

The pilotage of large vessels is an essential feature of safe navigation. In the above photograph, we see pilot tenders moored at the Liverpool cruise terminal whilst the two images on the right show tenders at work. The *Dunlin* (upper right) and *Puffin* (lower right) are used to take pilots to ships in the river, approach channels and the Mersey Bar. The pilot service was established in 1766 by the Liverpool Pilot Act which meant that it was compulsory to have a pilot aboard all ships in the Mersey. By 1858 the Mersey Docks and Harbour Board had assumed responsibility for the service under their Pilotage Committee but until 1988 the pilots remained self-employed or were employed by the shipping companies that regularly used the Mersey. The service operated with large pilot vessels from 1896 when a number of pilots were taken to the Bar or Anglesey each week and boarded vessels which were due to dock at the port. Pilots from vessels leaving the Port of Liverpool were transferred at the Bar and brought back to Liverpool by the pilot boat. However, it was decided in 1982 that the service would be better served by the use of fast launches like *Puffin* and *Dunlin* and the larger vessels were sold. One of these, the *Edmund Gardner*, is now preserved by the Merseyside Maritime Museum at Albert Dock.